# RAMADAN

## Joanna Ponto and Carol Gnojewski

**Enslow Publishing**
101 W. 23rd Street
Suite 240
New York, NY 10011
USA
enslow.com

*The editor would like to thank the Council on Islamic Education for their academic input*

Published in 2017 by Enslow Publishing, LLC.
101 W. 23rd Street, Suite 240, New York, NY 10011

**Library of Congress Cataloging-in-Publication Data**

Names: Ponto, Joanna, author.
Title: Ramadan / Joanna Ponto and Carol Gnojewski.
Description: New York : Enslow Publishing, 2017. | Series: The story of our holidays | Includes bibliographical references and index.
Identifiers: LCCN 2016022184| ISBN 9780766083523 (library bound) | ISBN 9780766083509 (pbk.) | ISBN 9780766083516 (6-pack)
Subjects: LCSH: Ramadan—Juvenile literature.
Classification: LCC BP186.4 .P66 2016 | DDC 297.3/62—dc23
LC record available at https://lccn.loc.gov/2016022184

Printed in China

**To Our Readers:** We have done our best to make sure all websites in this book were active and appropriate when we went to press. However, the author and the publisher have no control over and assume no liability for the material available on those websites or on any websites they may link to. Any comments or suggestions can be sent by e-mail to customerservice@enslow.com.

Portions of this book appeared in the book *Ramadan: A Muslim Time of Fasting, Prayer, and Celebration.*

**Photo Credits:** Cover, p. 1 Nidal Naseralla/Stockbyte/Getty Images; p. 4 Marco Vacca/Moment Mobile/Getty Images; p. 7 De Agostini Picture Library/Getty Images; p. 8 Robertus Pudyanto/Getty Images; p. 11 Anadolu Agency/Getty Images; p. 13 Pamela Smith/Corbis Documentary/Getty Images; p. 16 Distinctive Images/Shutterstock.com; p. 17 Lenar Musin/Shutterstock.com; p. 18 Arief Rasa/Moment/Getty Images; p. 20 rasoul ali/Moment/Getty Images; p. 22 Yuri Arcurs/DigitalVision/Getty Images; p. 23 Krzysztof Dydynski/Lonely Planet Images/Gertty Images; p. 25 Ameer Hamza/Moment/Getty Images; p. 27 bonchan/Shutterstock.com; p. 29 photo by Karen Huang.

# Contents

Muslims gather in a stadium in Milan, Italy, to say the last prayer of Ramadan together.

# Chapter 1

# Ninth Moon

There are nearly two billion Muslims— people of the Islamic faith—in the world. One special night each year, Muslim people across the globe scan the sky eagerly. At moonrise, Ramadan, the ninth month of the Islamic year, begins. During Ramadan, Muslims spend the entire month gathering as families and communities. They celebrate with prayer, fasts, and feasts in honor of God (*Allah* in Arabic).

September is the ninth month out of twelve months in the solar calendar year. Even though Ramadan is also the ninth of twelve months, it does not fall each year in September. In the Arabic language, the word *Ramadan* means the "hot month." However, Ramadan may fall in the summer or winter. This is because the Islamic calendar follows the lunar calendar, and the Western calendar follows the solar calendar.

# A Lunar Calendar

The solar calendar is based on the number of days it takes Earth to revolve around the sun. That is why there are 365 days in a solar year. The Islamic calendar, known as the Hijri (HIJ-ri) calendar depends on the motion of the moon. This makes it a lunar calendar.

The sun always lights half of the moon. It lights the half facing the sun. As the moon moves around Earth, we see different parts of it lit up. These are the moon's phases.

Muslims in olden days were great sky watchers and scientists. They noticed that a complete cycle of the moon lasts twenty-nine and a half days. Each set of phases equals one month. There are twelve cycles of twenty-nine and a half days, which makes a lunar year 354 days long. This matches what is written in the Quran, the Islamic holy book.

The lunar year is eleven days shorter than the solar calendar year. This is why lunar calendar months begin and end at different times.

The moon's first phase is the new moon. No moon can be seen. The moon first becomes visible as a crescent. Islamic months begin the day after the sighting of the first crescent moon.

The twelve months of the Islamic calendar are Muharram (moo-HUR-rum), Safar (SUF-er), Rabi (rub-EEY) the First, Rabi the Second, Jumada (joo-MAH-da) the First, Jumada the Second, Rajab (ra-JUB), Sha'ban (SHAA-bon), Ramadan (rah-ma-DAAN), Shawwaal (SHAW-waal), Zul Qi'dah (zool-KI-dah), and Zul Hijja (zool-HEEJ-jah).

As the moon moves around Earth, we see different parts of it lit up. Sometimes we see no moon. Other times, we may see a crescent moon, a half moon, or a full moon.

# Eyes on the Sky

On the night before Ramadan, moon watchers wait. With telescopes and binoculars, they look for the moon. Children in Egypt carry a *fanoos* (faa-NOOS), or lantern. A fanoos is made of tin and colored glass. It has a candle inside of it. Lighting a fanoos during Ramadan is a tradition that began more than a thousand years ago.

This Indonesian Muslim is studying the moon. Muslims use telescopes to help them determine the beginning and end of Ramadan.

# Chapter 2

# The Message of Islam

Calendars tend to be arranged around important events in history. The Christian calendar centers on the life and death of Jesus Christ. Time before the birth of Jesus is often called BC, which means "before Christ." Dates after Jesus's birth are labeled AD (*Anno Domini*)—"in the Year of Our Lord." It has been in use in many countries around the world since 1582. The Christian calendar was adopted for nonreligious purposes, too. To make the calendar useful to everyone, the terms "before the common era" (BCE) and "common era" (CE) were created. BCE can be used in place of BC, and CE can be used in place of AD.

# The Islamic Calendar

The Islamic calendar centers on the formation of the first Muslim community in Medina (also spelled Madinah). It was made in 638 CE by Muslims who believed they were part of the history begun by Muhammad's teachings about Islam. Dates on the Islamic calendar start from the year that the Prophet Muhammad moved from the city of Mecca (also spelled Makkah) to Medina in the year 622 CE. This event is called the Hijra (HIJ-ra). Dates are labeled AH, which means "after Hijra." Islamic dates are 579 years behind Western dates. The year 2017 CE, for example, is the year 1438 AH.

The Prophet Muhammad lived in what is now Saudi Arabia, a country in the Middle East. During the time of Muhammad, Arabs lived in tribes. Wars and fights among tribes went on all the time. Most tribal people worshipped many gods and goddesses. Muhammad chose instead to worship Allah, the one god of his ancestor Abraham. Muhammad was orphaned at the age of six. His uncle, Abu Talib, raised him in the city of Mecca. When Muhammad was young, he worked as a shepherd. Later, Muhammad married a wealthy businesswoman named Khadijah.

## Hira Cave

Every year during the month of Ramadan, Muhammad would travel to a cave called Hira (HEE-ra) in the hills near Mecca. According to Muslim belief, he went there to be alone with God and to pray for guidance. The angel Gabriel appeared before Muhammad when he was forty years old. This visitation happened near the end of

Thousands of pilgrims visit Hira cave, where Muhammad went to meditate and heard the first revelations of the Quran.

Ramadan. In Arabic, the word "angel" is *malaa'ika* (ma-LAA-e-kaa). It means "conveyor," or "carrier." Muslims believe that angels are servants of God.

Angels are believed to be invisible to humans. They are thought to surround people at all times to guide and protect them. Gabriel is a special angel. His job is to give messages from God to holy people called prophets.

## A Message from God

When Gabriel appeared before him, Muhammad became very frightened. Gabriel gave Muhammad the first of many messages. The angel asked him to read a verse that now appears in the Quran. But Muhammad did not know how to read or to write. The angel embraced him and told him again to read, and so Muhammad did.

When Muhammad received the message from Gabriel, he hurried home to Khadijah. He repeated what the angel had told him. Together, they asked her cousin, a scholar, for advice. He convinced Muhammad to accept the revelation that Gabriel had brought him.

Muhammad memorized God's words and presented them to the tribal leaders. Muhammad's message about worshipping one god and living peacefully was unpopular. The leaders did not want to change the traditions that made them powerful. But many other people liked what Muhammad had to say. The Muslim population spread and outlasted the warring tribes. Now, Islam is the fastest-growing religion in the world.

Muhammad recited the message of Islam to all who would listen. Scribes wrote down these teachings. Before Muhammad's death, they were organized into a

According to Muslim tradition, the angel Gabriel brought God's messages to Muhammad for twenty-three years. These revelations are organized into 114 chapters in the Quran.

holy book called the Quran. The Quran is the primary source of Islamic teaching. Like the Christian Bible and the Jewish Torah, it is said to be the word of God. Written in verse form, the Quran reads like poetry. Speaking it aloud makes its graceful language more powerful.

Because Muhammad received the first passages of the Quran during Ramadan, it is a holy month for Muslims. Ramadan is sometimes called the Month of the Quran. The twenty-seventh night of the month is celebrated as the night he received his first revelation. It is called Laylat-al-Qadr (LAY-lat-al-CUD-er). This means "Night of Decree." The Quran is important because its teachings are part of a Muslim's daily life. In some Muslim countries, businesses and schools close on the twenty-seventh day. This lets worshippers rest during the day to prepare for a night of prayer.

# Chapter 3

# Praying to Mecca

Muslims spend Ramadan thinking about life, and they also spend time alone with God, like Muhammad in his cave. Muslims pray to God five times a day. These prayers are called *salat* (sa-LAAT). At dawn, midday, late afternoon, sunset, and in the evening, Muslims take time for ritual prayer.

## Facing Mecca

During prayer, Muslims face toward the Ka'bah (KAA-bah), a cube-shaped building located in the holy city Mecca. Muslims believe it was built as a house of worship by Abraham and his son Ishmael long ago. The direction of the prayer (facing the Ka'bah) is called *qibla* (KIB-la). The qibla varies depending on where one lives. In order to find the qibla, many Muslims use a prayer compass. This special compass looks like an ordinary compass. But, instead of pointing north, it points to Mecca. There are even prayer compass watches. These watches can automatically calculate prayer times, too. Prayer calendars and software programs also help to remind Muslims of their prayer schedules. This is important because Muslims live all over the world and in many different time zones.

One way that Muslims show their commitment to God is by going to a mosque and bowing to God in worship.

This woman used a prayer compass to tell her in which direction to pray.

## Place of Prayer

Before prayer, Muslims perform a washing ritual called *wudu* (wo-DOO). During wudu, Muslims cleanse their hands, mouth, nose, face, arms, and feet. This prepares Muslims for worship. Muslims stand, raise their arms, sit, kneel, and bow before God as they pray.

The word "mosque" (MAHSK) comes from *masjid* (MUS-jid), a place for bowing low. "Muslim" means "submitter to God."

The prayer area in a mosque is a simple open space, usually carpeted. Special mats or prayer rugs are used to mark the rows that worshippers form when praying together.

Most mosques have a large area where people can kneel and pray.

Prayer services increase throughout Ramadan. Muslims may spend all day or night in prayer. Muslims are encouraged to pray together rather than alone whenever possible.

Muslims often pray together at a mosque. A mosque is a sacred place, like a church or a synagogue. An imam (ee-MAAM), or prayer leader, gives a sermon on Fridays. He leads prayer by reciting verses from the Quran in a songlike way. The other worshippers follow the imam as he bows before God.

On each corner of a mosque stand tall, slender towers, or minarets (mihn-uh-REHTS). A caller, or *mu'adhin* (moo-ED-dhin), calls from the minaret to gather people for worship. The mu'adhin may use a microphone and a loudspeaker that reaches across town. In Cairo, Egypt, a cannon is fired to announce the Ramadan prayers.

The inside of a mosque is organized and is simple. There are no statues and paintings inside a mosque. Instead, mosques are decorated with calligraphy and patterns of colorful tiles. Large courtyards and prayer halls may contain thick carpets, fountains, arches, and pillars. The Prophet's Mosque has enormous electronic umbrellas in one of its courtyards. These umbrellas open when it rains to keep worshippers dry.

Some mosques hold an *itekaf* (it-e-KAF) as the month draws to a close. In Arabic, *itekaf* means "seclusion." It is a spiritual retreat that gives Muslims a chance to think about their goals and to become closer to God. Along with *taraweeh* (tur-ah-WEE-uh), or special night prayers in Ramadan, itekaf gives Muslims a chance to be with their fellow worshippers to share meals, to talk, and to learn from each other. For some Muslims, this night of togetherness builds excitement for the festive Eid ul-Fitr that takes place after Ramadan.

Some mosques have smooth, flat stone roofs, while others have large painted or tiled domes called *qubbas* (KOOB-bas). The Prophet's Mosque, shown here, is a famous mosque in Medina, Saudi Arabia.

# Chapter 4

# Fasting for Ramadan

One of the key ways Muslims observe Ramadan is through *sawm* (SO-um), or fasting. They cannot eat or drink anything during daylight hours. Muslims rise before dawn and eat a hearty breakfast, or *sahur* (su-HOOR). Then, they do not eat or drink again until nighttime. The Quran says that followers may eat and drink at any time during the night.

Our bodies can survive without water for three or four days. You can survive without food for many weeks. It all depends on how much fat and muscle you have. Even so, think about all of the times that you eat meals or snacks during the day. Going without food and water for a whole day is a big sacrifice. When Ramadan falls in the summer, a daily fast may last for twelve hours because the days are longer. Sacrifice is part of

Children do not have to fast all month until they are teenagers. In some Muslim families, young children may skip a meal on weekends or fast for a few hours each day.

what Ramadan is about. It helps Muslims appreciate how lucky they are to have enough food to eat every day. It reminds them that others are not so lucky.

Another Ramadan duty is *zakat* (za-KAT). Zakat is giving money to help the poor. Some children who do not fast give their allowance to the poor instead. Thinking of others is part of the Ramadan spirit.

## Iftar

Once night falls, Muslim cities come alive. After night prayers, Ramadan becomes a time for food and fun. A snack of dates and water is eaten to break the fast. Then, a large evening meal called *iftar* (if-TAAR) is served.

Cafes and restaurants that were closed during the day reopen at night. They fill with hungry customers. Hotels may set up outdoor tents with popular foods and fruit drinks. There may be music and dancing. Families and friends visit each other and have parties and get-togethers. Sports such as soccer and rugby are played in lighted fields or in the streets.

People often come together to break their fast at the end of the day during Ramadan.

# Chapter 5

# The Eid Festival Arrives

Ramadan ends on the first day of the month of Shawwaal. Sky watchers once again watch for a crescent moon. When a crescent appears, the new month has arrived. Eid ul-Fitr (EED-ul-FIT-er) begins. The Eid is a three-day festival to celebrate a successful fast. In rural villages in Yemen, fires are lit to announce the joyful Eid tidings. Families then prepare for community Eid prayers.

After prayers, gifts are exchanged. Neighbors and friends bring each other wrapped cakes, nuts, and strings of dried fruit such as figs, dates, apricots, and raisins. They congratulate each other for completing the fast. "Eid Mubarak" (EED moo-BAA-rek), they say. Happy Festival! You can try the apricot honey tart recipe inspired by Ramadan on page 27.

In countries like Pakistan, there are street fairs with balloons and carnival games. Street vendors, people who offer goods for sale, paint their carts bright green, blue, and gold. They add symbols such as

This woman is making a special dish for Eid, called sheer korma. It is made from lentils, which she needs to clean and remove the skins from.

stars and crescent moons to represent Islam. There may be parades with sword-dancing and drums.

Wherever Muslims gather to celebrate Eid, it is a time for relaxation and merriment. Communities make sure that everyone, including poor people, is well fed and content. Muslims around the world happily give thanks to God for their health, their strength, and their opportunities in life.

# Cooking During Ramadan
## Apricot and Honey Tart

### Ingredients:

1 large puff pastry sheet
12 fresh apricots, cleaned and cut into segments
1 teaspoon (5 mL) nutmeg

⅓ cup (80 mL) honey
½ cup (75 g) chopped walnuts or almonds
¼ cup (60 mL) raspberry jam
zest of one lemon
dried cherries for garnish (optional)

### Directions:

1. Preheat oven to 350°F (177°C). Grease a 9-by-11-inch (23-by-28-centimeter) pie dish with butter.
2. Gently unfold the puff pastry. Use a rolling pin to smooth out any creases left by the folding. Gently place the puff pastry over the pie dish and press down into the corners of the dish with your fingers. There might be a little too much dough, and pieces may hang off the edge. Just cut them off and discard. Gently pierce the bottom of the crust with a fork.
3. Using a spoon, spread the jam on the uncooked crust. Be gentle. You don't want to tear the dough, but you do want an even layer.
4. In a large bowl, combine the apricot, nutmeg, honey, nuts, and lemon zest. Stir until all the apricots and nuts are coated in honey and spices.
5. Pour the apricots into the pie dish. Spread around to make sure that they are evenly layered. You can even arrange the top layer of apricots into a crescent moon or into circles if you'd like. Drizzle with a bit more honey and top with dried cherries, if desired.
6. Bake for about 20 minutes, or until the pastry around the edge of the pie dish is golden in color or the apricots are soft when poked with a fork.
7. Serve at room temperature during iftar.

**\* Adult supervision required.**

# Ramadan Craft

Ramadan starts when we see a crescent moon in the ninth month of the Islamic calendar. Make a Ramadan decoration using the moon and stars.

## Here are the supplies you will need:

tracing paper
10 sheets of white paper
gold crayons or markers
silver crayons or markers
scissors
hole punch
8 feet of string or yarn

## Directions:

1. Draw a star on a piece of paper. This will be your pattern. Trace the star pattern using tracing paper. Cut out the traced star pattern. Trace as many stars as you can fit onto another sheet of paper. Color the stars silver and cut them out. Do the same thing with a moon pattern. Color the moons gold and cut them out.

2. Using the hole punch, punch a small hole near the top of each star and each moon.

3. String one star, then one moon onto yarn. Repeat, spacing the stars and moons evenly.

4. Ask an adult to help you hang your Ramadan decoration over a door.

# Stars and Moons Garland

*Safety Note: Be sure to ask for
help from an adult, if needed,
to complete this project.

# Glossary

calligraphy  An elegant, artistic style of handwriting.

decree  A religious order.

Islam  The religious faith of Muslims that is based on the belief in one God, known in Arabic as Allah.

mosque  A building used by Muslims for public worship; comes from the Arabic word *masjid*.

Muslim  A believer in the religion of Islam.

prophet  A person who delivers a message that is believed to have come from God.

Quran  The book of sacred writings accepted by Muslims as revelations from God.

revelation  Something that is revealed by God to humans.

ritual  An established religious ceremony.

scribe  A person who copies writing.

sermon  A religious speech.

worship  To honor or to show respect to God or to a sacred object.

# Learn More

## Books

Faruqi, Reem. *Lailah's Lunchbox: A Ramadan Story*. Thomaston, ME: Tilbury House Publishers, 2015.

Khanam, Farida. *Ramadan: The Month of Fasting*. Chennai, India: Goodword Books, 2014.

Robert, Na'ima. *Ramadan Moon*. London, UK: Francis Lincoln Children's Books, 2015.

## Websites

**The Life of Muhammad**
*www.pbs.org/muhammad/timeline_html.shtml*
Learn more about the Prophet of Islam, Muhammad.

**Ramadan: PBS Kids**
*pbskids.org/arthur/holiday/scrapbook/ramadan.html*
Learn more about Ramadan from Arthur and his friends.

**Ramadan on the Net**
*www.holidays.net/ramadan*
Find out more about Ramadan from this website.

# Index